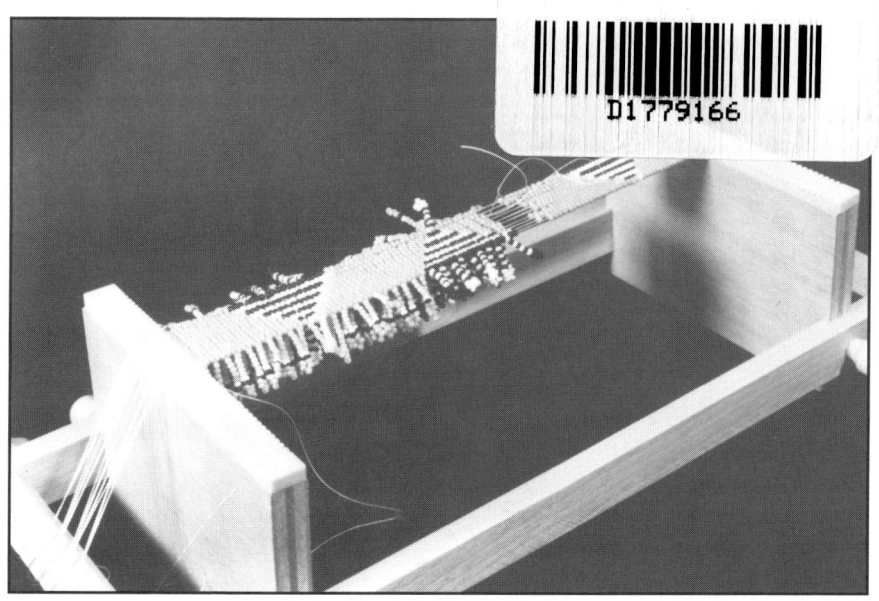

Defining Some Words

Base beads: These strands of beads form the underside surface to which the stem beads are attached. These beads are strung on the warp.

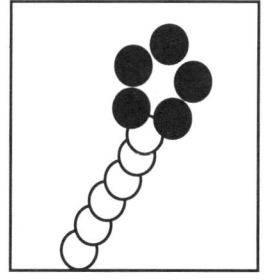

Stem and loop

Stem and loop beads: the beads which stick up from the base beads forming rows of fringe. Stems may have a loop of one or more beads at the top. These beads are strung on the weft or weaving thread.

Warp thread: the long threads which are stretched across the loom from end to end; a <u>pair</u> of warp threads will be inside each strand of beads in the base.

Weft thread: this is your weaving thread. It is passed between the warp threads and through the stem beads using a needle.

Overview: Beads are added to both warp and weft. Rows of stems or fringes are added as weaving is done.

A Basic Loom
(Top Down View)

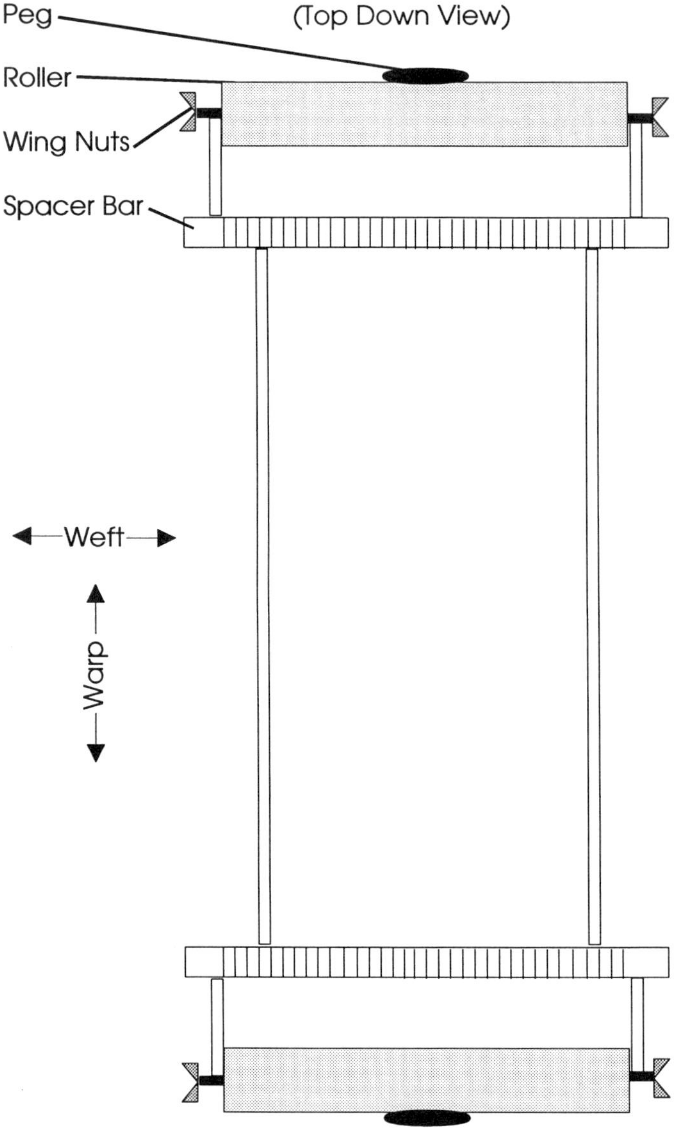

- Peg
- Roller
- Wing Nuts
- Spacer Bar
- Weft
- Warp

Fig. 1. The basic loom.

     Many different kinds of looms are available but most have the same basic parts. On some, the spacer bar will be a wire coil, on others it will be a piece of wood or plastic with grooves in it which evenly separates the warp threads. Looms with rollers are the easiest to work with because they allow you to adjust the tension on the warp threads.

Contemporary Beadwork II: Sea Anemone Beadwork

A Three-Dimensional Loomed Beadwork Technique

by Diane Fitzgerald

Copyright 1995 by Diane M. Fitzgerald.

All rights reserved. No part of this book may be reproduced by any means, graphic, electronic or mechanical, including photocopying, recording, taping, or information storage and retrieval systems whether for sale or free distribution.

Published by
Beautiful Beads
115 Hennepin Avenue
Minneapolis, MN 55401
612-333-0170
Fax: 612-333-8122

*This book is dedicated to
Horace Goodhue
of
St. Paul, Minnesota*

ISBN 0-9646077-1-9

About the author:

Diane Fitzgerald is a bead artist who works in a variety of contemporary bead assemblage techniques, including what is traditionally considered beadwork using seed beads, and bead assemblage with larger beads. Since 1989, she has taught a wide range of bead classes at her shop, Beautiful Beads, in Minneapolis, Minnesota and around the country. As a bead collector,  she specializes in contemporary art glass beads, particularly American, European and Japanese. She has spent time in the Czech Republic and Germany learning about the glass bead industry and meeting beadmakers there.

Other books by this author:
"Beads and Threads: A New Technique for Fiber Jewelry," with coauthor Helen Banes; published by Flower Valley Press, 1993.
"Contemporary Beadwork I: Counted and Charted Patterns for Flat Peyote Stitch," 1995; self-published.

The Story of
Sea Anemone Beadwork

by Diane Fitzgerald

Sea Anemone Beadwork is a name I've given to type of loomed, three-dimensional beadwork with stems or rows of fringes which stand up from a base of beads. The technique results in a piece which resembles a sea anemone, a flowerlike, undersea creature whose petals flow with the movement of surrounding water.

Like many pieces of beadwork, there's a story behind this one. Although I wish I could take credit for inventing this technique, I can only take credit for reinventing it and passing it along to you. Here's how I found out about it.

Shortly after I opened my shop, Beautiful Beads, in downtown Minneapolis, I began to study Horace Goodhue's book "Indian Bead-Weaving Patterns." Although a copy of his book had been on my shelf for several years, I hadn't really sat down to work with it. I knew that he lived in St. Paul, just across the MIssissippi River, so I called him one day. He pleasantly told me he had just started an evening class in beadwork and that I would be welcome to join it.

Horace was born in 1904 and has been interested in beadwork since he was a child. He has collected patterns and examples of beadwork from Native American's across the United States and added new techniques to his book with each revision. Although not a Native American himself, he has always been close to this community and has a high degree of respect for them and their art, particularly their beadwork. He tries to encourage young Native Americans to continue their traditions in any of the many forms.

At each class Horace had showed us some of his pieces. Still there were drawers and cases full of beadwork that we hadn't seen. One evening he brought out an unusual piece of beadwork. It looked like a porcupine or spiny creature of some sort.

It was found in his mother's jewelry box with other keepsakes and medals after she died. By appearance and condition it was obviously a very old piece. Although his mother had known he was interested in beadwork, she had never showed it to him. He surmised that perhaps his mother, born and raised in the early days of Minnesota, had had a Native American friend who had given her the piece. I like to ponder how it was made because the piece is truly unique in its construction. Although Horace had made a piece similar to it many years ago, he could not recollect how he had done it.

The piece had a two-inch square base made of several strands of beads. Standing up from the base were stems of beads with loops on the ends. The main color was coral and it had accents of white, black, gold and turquoise blue. This base was attached to a band which adds to the mystery. It is an eight-bead diagonal weave, an old and rare pattern which Horace has traced to Canadian Cree work. He first learned it in a "pattern trade" with an elderly Ojibwa-Cree grandmother on the Red Lake Reservation in northern Minnesota. Not knowing its history, he describes the technique as "Red Lake Zig-Zag" in his book, "Indian Bead-Weaving Patterns."

How ever it was made, the piece was now very fragile and some of the threads were starting to fray and break. Horace could see how absolutely delighted I was with the wiggly little piece and generously offered to loan it to me so that I could figure out how it was constructed. I hesitated, but I couldn't resist. He found a snug little box for it and it went into my purse. (I knew it would take sheer will power to return it, but I'm happy to say I overcame my baser instincts and did return it.)

Figuring out its construction wasn't easy at all. Using a powerful magnifying glass, I could see that each strand of beads in the base had a pair of threads running through it. By gently prying apart the beads with a pin--very gently! -- I could see that a weft thread went between this pair of threads and through the stems. At first I tried to construct the piece without a loom, but was not successful. Having done beadwork on a loom as a child, I soon realized that using a loom would have to be part of the solution.

One morning, I woke up and could see clearly in my mind how the piece was constructed. I must have been unconsciously thinking about the problem all night. There was nothing more in the world that I wanted to do that day than start that piece. I called work (At the time, I worked full-time in public relations.) to say that I was taking a vacation day and got started.

I had all the things I needed to begin: my bead loom from childhood, the familiar Walco Bead Loom, thread, needles and beads. By 7 a.m. I was well on the way to stringing up the loom. I tied on my first weft thread and strung one of the little "stems" and passed the needle through the first pair of warp threads. It seemed just natural for the stem to fall forward and hang down between the warp threads so that I was working on the wrong side of the piece. Near midnight that same day, bleary-eyed, I finished my first "Sea Anemone" piece and called it "Pink Anemone." Only the finishing, weaving the ends in and adding a clasp, was left.

That first piece was about two inches square with a base of pink opalescsent beads lined with red. The stems are similar beads but in blue-green and the loops at the top of the stem are pink topped by a single clear bright red bead. The piece looks like red points of light on a pink bed, but when it falls open the pale blue-green stems complement the loop colors on top.

My second piece, a bracelet called Confetti Anemone, has black beads in the base and the stems. The loops are multi-colored silver-lined beads in red, pink, lavender, light blue, royal blue, blue-green, green, yellow and clear each picked up at random.

Since those first attempts, I have made several pieces in the Sea Anemone technique. Some of the bracelets remind people of a caterpillar and everyone loves to stroke the soft coolness of the beads. Now it's your turn to make your own "Sea Anemone" piece and luxuriate in the feel of the beads as they glide through your fingers!

Followup: A few years after Horace loaned me this piece, he was driving in the Southwest with his wife. When she said she smelled smoke, they jumped out of their van. Within minutes, the van went up in flames. With it went the original piece of beadwork he loaned to me which he had with him for safekeeping. If there is a moral to this story, it may be that sharing our beadwork techniques enables them to be continued. We can all appreciate Horace Goodhue's lifetime of generosity.

Creating Your Own Sea Anemone Bracelet

Step 1. What You Need to Get Started

Selecting Your Beads: Size 11° round seed beads work best. Beads smaller than this are difficult to work with because of the number of times the thread must pass through the hole. You will need about two ounces in two or more colors: one color for the base, one or more for the stems and one or more for the loops.

Selecting Your Thread: Nymo "D" thread on the spool, made by the Belding Company is a very strong nylon thread. It is available in black and white. Use only thread from a spool (not a bobbin) because it is heavier. You should consider the color of the thread you use because it will change the color of transparent beads and show slightly between other beads, changing the overall effect.

Selecting Your Needles: I prefer to use size 12 Sharps needles, a short needle, since only one bead is picked up at a time. It is not necessary to use the long beading needles which bend easily and are more expensive. You will need at least two needles.

Selecting Your Loom: Several types of bead looms are available or you can make your own. It is convenient to have a loom which allows you to tighten your warp threads. A good quality loom makes work easier. Wire looms are not recommended

Other Items Needed: A small sharp scissor, clear nail polish to coat the knots, a Bic lighter, a small piece of leather or ultra suede, a large snap fastener or other closure and leather glue such as Barge Cement from Tandy Leather Co. or E-6000 glue.

Directions are given for a bracelet to fit a seven-inch wrist. Adjust as needed to fit your wrist.

Sources of supplies and other recommended books are listed at the back of this book.

Step 2. Stringing up the Loom

1. Creating the Base: The base consists of 6 or more columns of beads strung with a double warp thread through them. Using the Nymo D thread, measure a piece of thread 50 inches long (or 2 1/2 times the length of your loom), pass it through the needle and bring the two ends together so they are even. Tape the ends to the table.

Fig. 2. Strands of base beads strung and laid out, ready to go on the loom.

2. String 6 1/2" of beads (or enought beads to equal the circumference of your wrist less 1/2") on the double warp thread. Cut the thread near the needle and remove the needle. Tape both ends to the table. String six or more strands in this way and lay them out side by side. Use as many strands as you wish to make your bracelet wider. (Each strand of beads will have two threads running through it.) The beads may be all one color, each strand may be a different color creating stripes, or you may create a pattern. Try to select beads that are uniform in size.

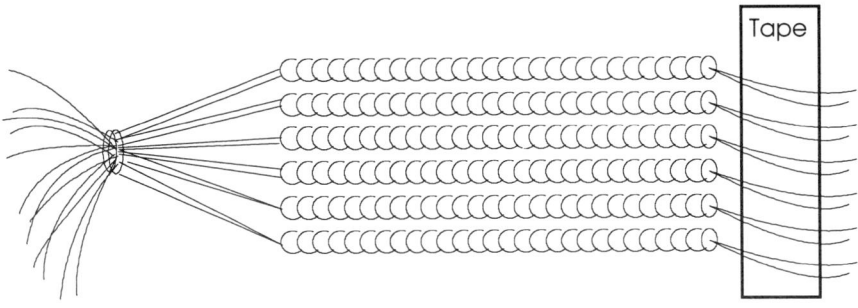

Fig. 3. The strands of beads tied together with an overhand knot.

3. Remove the tape from the threads at one end. Tie all strands of thread at one end together in an overhand knot. (Fig. 3) Do the same to the other end positioning the knot so that you can hook it over the peg at the other end.

4. Hook one knot over the peg at one end of the bead loom and the other knot over the peg at the other end. Position warp pairs evenly across the spacer bar at both ends of the loom. Be sure the warp pairs lie perpendicular to the spacer bars at both ends. One pair of threads will be in each space on the spacer bar.

5. Rotate the roller as necessary to tighten the warps. Tighten the wing nuts firmly to maintain tension. Warps should be firm but not overly tight or your piece will not be fexible when removed from the loom. Position your loom so the working end is closest to you.

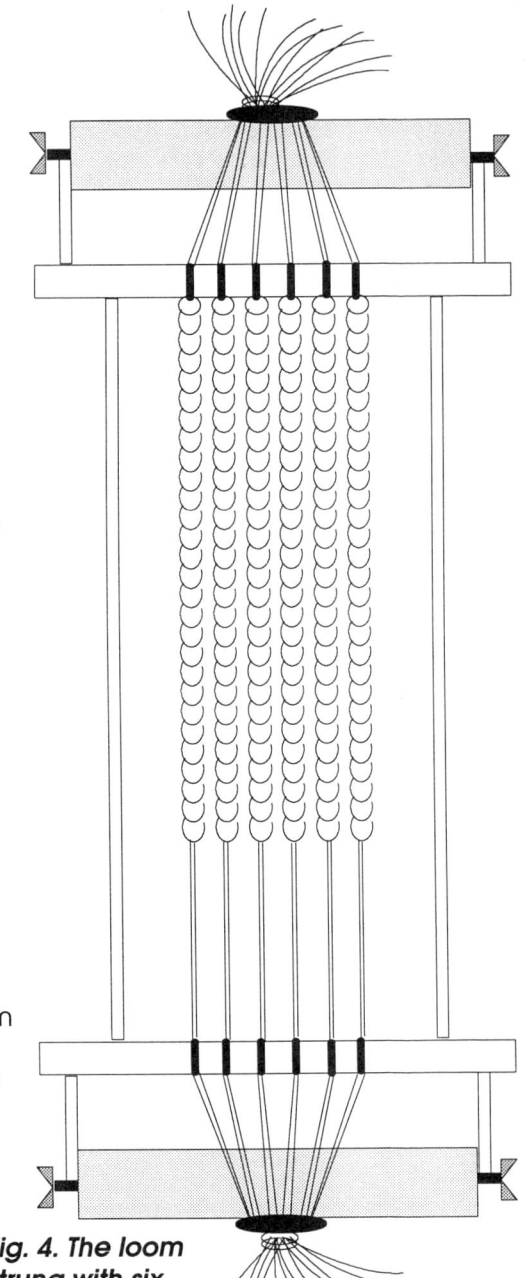

Fig. 4. The loom strung with six warp pairs with beads on the warps.

Overhand Knot

Step 3. Weaving

1. String a needle with 1 1/2 yds. of Nymo thread. Tie one end of the thread to the outside warp pair leaving a 6" tail which will be hidden later. Work with a single thread now.

2. Begin with three rows of plain loom weaving. Put five beads on the needle (one bead between each warp pair) and bring it up under the warp threads so that one bead is between each pair of warp threads. Bring the thread through the beads on the underside of the warp threads (Fig. 5), then pass the thread back through the beads on the top of the warp threads, going in the opposite direction (Fig. 6). It helps to push the beads gently up from the bottom with your index finger so that your needle will pass through the top of the bead hole and not pierce the thread already in the hole. Slide this row of beads close to the spacer bar. Do three rows in this manner. Knot weaving thread around the outer warp pair before beginning stems. Always keep the base beads packed tightly together so they are nearly touching.

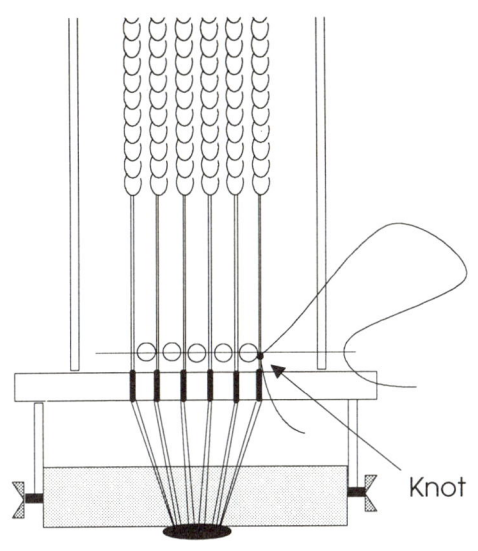

Fig. 5. Weaving thread tied to outside warp pair and beads positioned between each warp pair. Needle moves right to left, under the warp pairs.

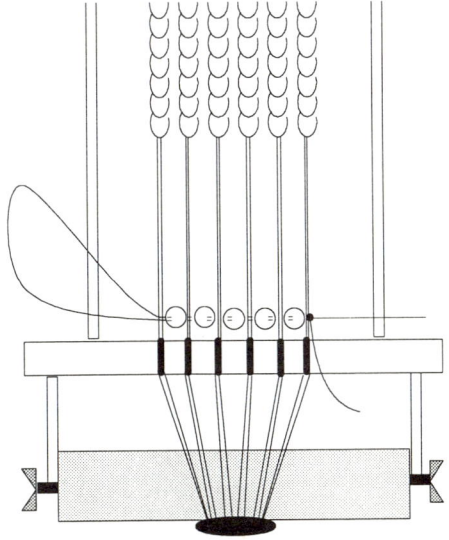

Fig. 6. Needle is passed left to right, through the beads and then back over the warp pairs.

3. Creating a stem and loop. With your thread still attached to the loomwork, string 7 Color A beads (stems) on the thread and five of Color B (loops). Pass the thread back through the stem beads, towards the warp (Fig. 8). Slide the beads along the thread so that the stem beads are close to the warp threads (Fig. 9).

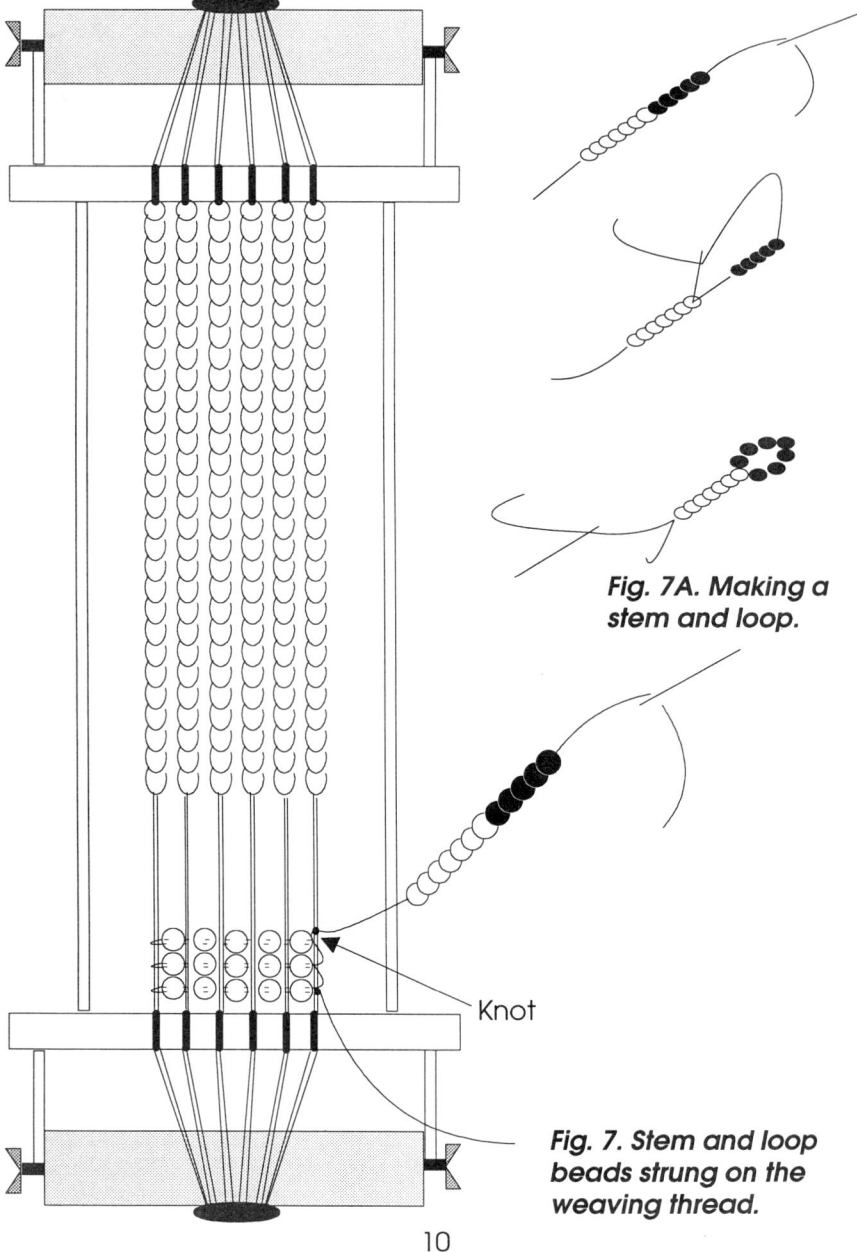

Fig. 7A. Making a stem and loop.

Fig. 7. Stem and loop beads strung on the weaving thread.

Stem colors: Stems usually consist of 7 or more beads and a loop of 4-6 beads. When the piece lies flat, the loop beads show the most. When the piece is bent, the beads at the base of the stem pop into view. Consider this in selecting your colors. You may want a dark color to set off the bright colors in the loops, or you may want darker loops with a bright color as a surprise when the piece is flexed or moved.

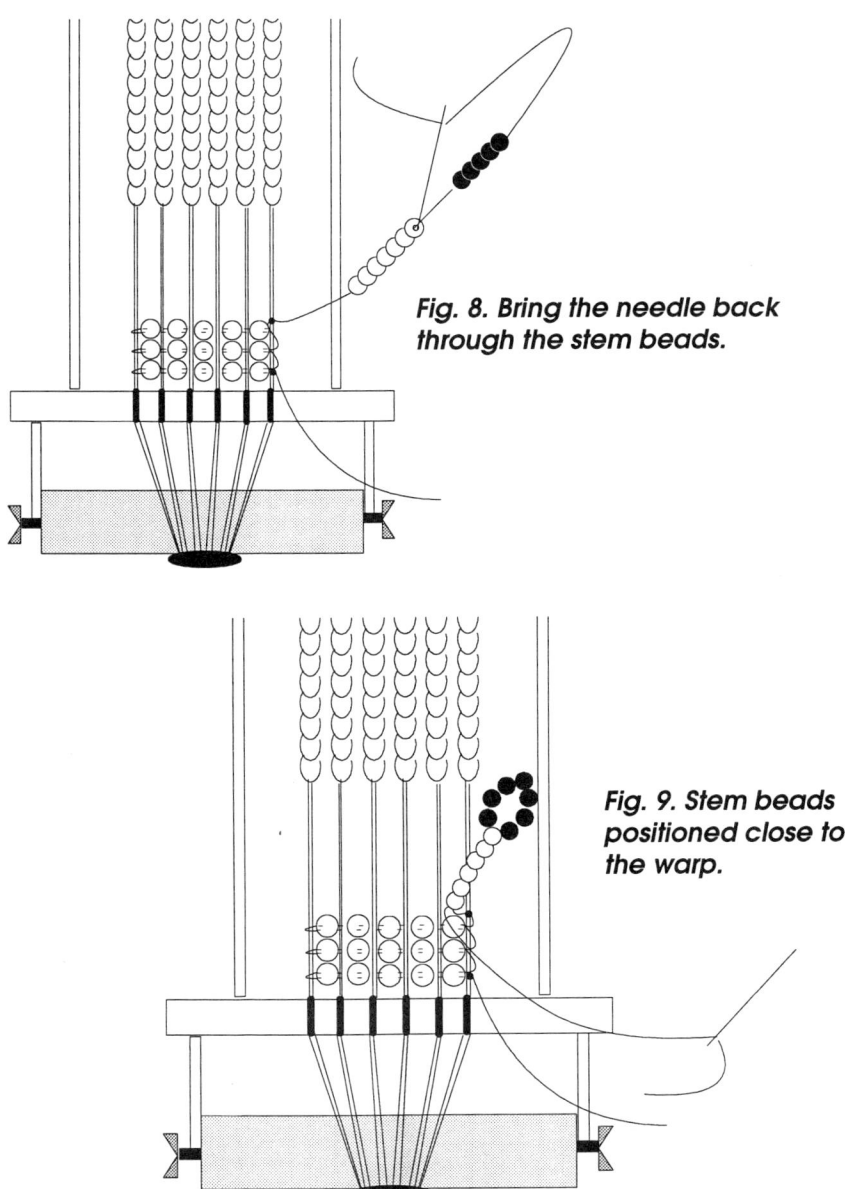

Fig. 8. Bring the needle back through the stem beads.

Fig. 9. Stem beads positioned close to the warp.

4. Push the stem so it hangs downward between the first and second warp pairs. Part the second pair of warp threads and pass the needle between them so that your needle comes out on top of the warps (Fig. 10). Make another stem. Then pass the needle between the third pair of warp threads. Push the arm so that it hangs down in the space between the first and second warp threads. Continue to make one stem for each space between the pairs of warp threads across the loom from right to left.

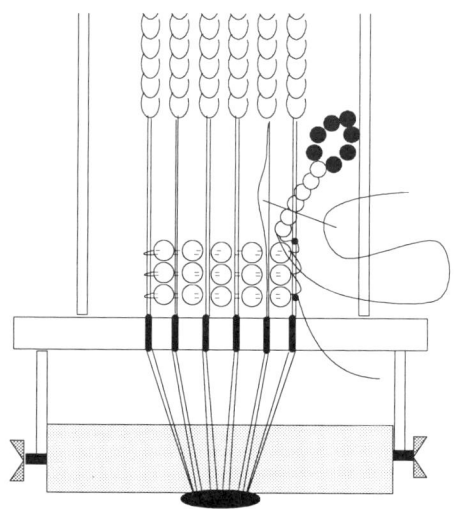

Fig. 10. Part the warp pair with your thumbnail and pass the needle between the two threads of the warp pair so that your needle comes out on top.

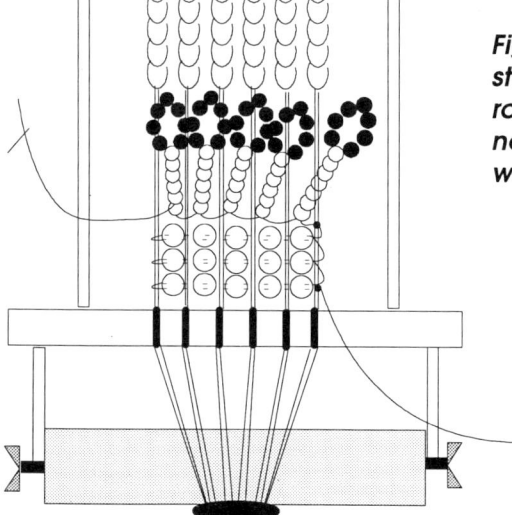

Fig. 11. Continue making stems and loops across the row, after each, pass the needle between the next warp pair.

5. After making a stem between the last two warp pairs, slide two beads toward you along the warp and pass the needle through these two beads going forward or away from your work (Fig. 12).

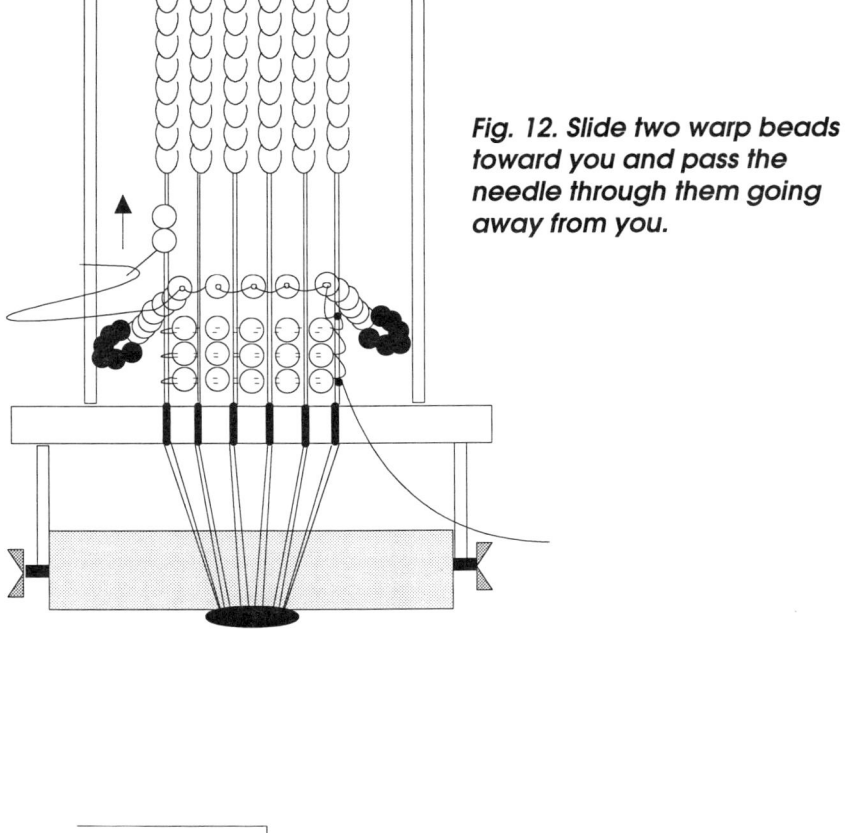

Fig. 12. Slide two warp beads toward you and pass the needle through them going away from you.

Fig. 12A. This is the route your needle will follow in stringing rows of arms.

6. Push two beads along each warp close to the row of stems just finished. Continue to make stems across the row, from left to right, then right to left. Between each row of stems, push two beads into place along each warp pair when a row is completed. <u>Important!</u> As you work, continually push your warp beads together toward you so they are almost touching.

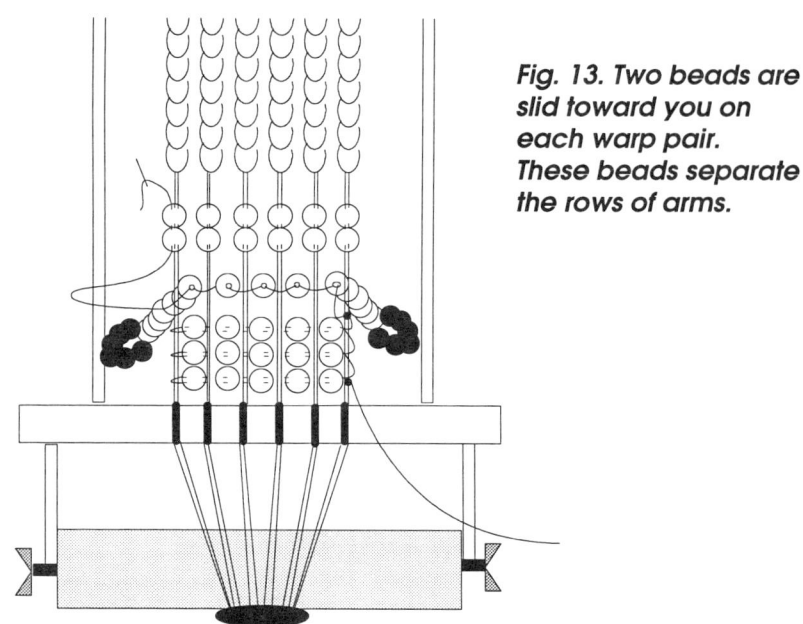

Fig. 13. Two beads are slid toward you on each warp pair. These beads separate the rows of arms.

Fig. 14. Side View of the Loom: Note that the stems hang down between the warp threads and some beads are pushed over the spacer bar to allow more space for weaving. You may wish to place a piece of removable tape over the extra beads on the warp to keep them out of the way.

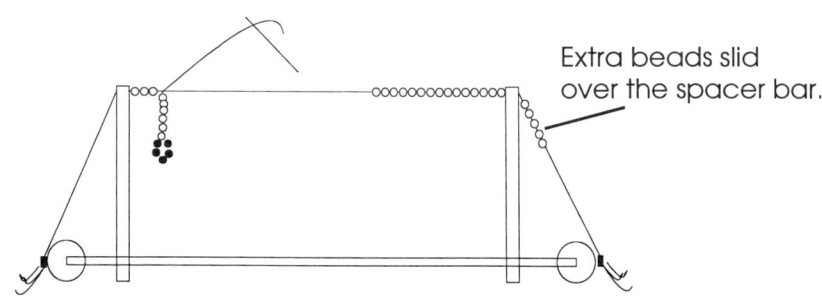

Extra beads slid over the spacer bar.

7. Adding New Thread: Stop weaving when you still have about four inches left. <u>Do not remove the needle.</u> Just let this threaded needle hang for now. String up a <u>new</u> needle with thread. Tie a double overhand knot in the end of the thread. Trim the end and melt it with a lighter or coat the knot with clear nail polish. Bring this thread through two to four warp beads in the completed work so that it comes out near your old thread (Fig. 15). Let the knot in your new thread slip inside a bead if possible. Tie the old thread and the new thread together with a square knot (Fig. 16). Pass the old thread through several warp beads before clipping it off. Dab your knot with clear nail polish. Now you have a new needle and thread to work with.

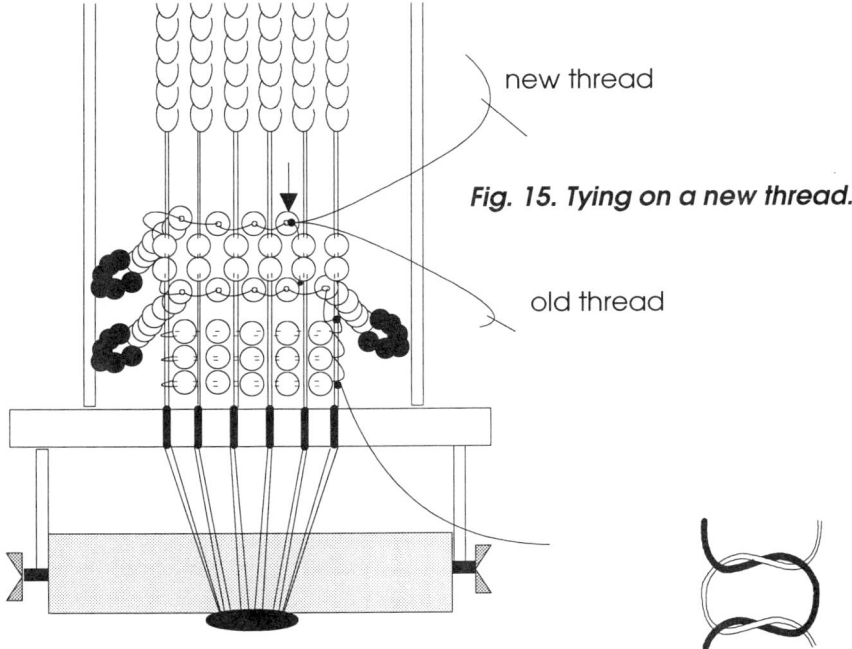

Fig. 15. Tying on a new thread.

Fig. 16. Square Knot: Left thread goes over the right thread and around it. Then the right thread goes over the left thread and passes through the loop.

8. When your work measures 6" including the plain weaving, slide the remaining beads out of the way and do three or four rows of plain bead weaving as described in Step 5, making your piece 6 1/2" total in length. One/half inch will be added with the closure. Knot your weaving thread around the warp outside warp pair. Bury your beginning and ending weaving thread in nearby beads.

Step 4: Finishing and Adding a Closure:

1. Although there are many ways to make a closure, the following closure is comfortable, easy to do and materials are readily available. Select soft leather or Ultrasuede in a color that works with your beads. Measure two pieces of leather or ultrasuede that are two inches long and one-half inch wider than your bracelet. (The piece will be trimmed later.) Fold in half and mark the fold line on the wrong side so that each half is one inch.

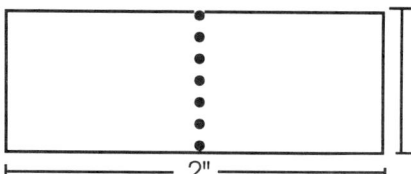

Fig. 17. Cut two pieces of leather two inches long and the width of bracelet base plus 1/2".

2. Check the length of your work to be sure it will be the correct length after the closure is added. Remove the warp threads from one end of the loom and untie the knot. Handle the piece carefully. Remove any excess beads from the warp pairs. Starting at the center, string the center pair of warp threads into a needle. Pull these threads through the leather at the midpoint of the centerline. The warp threads should go into the center of the leather from the right side and come out on the wrong side. Remove the needle and string the next pair of warp threads into it. Pull these threads through the leather the same way, but about one bead-width away from the first set of threads and along the center line. Continue to pull all pairs of warp threads through the leather. Tie pair #1 to pair #3, pair #2 to pair #4, etc. until all are tied together. Be careful not to pull the thread too tightly. Dab the knots with nail polish and when dry trim 1/4" from the knots.

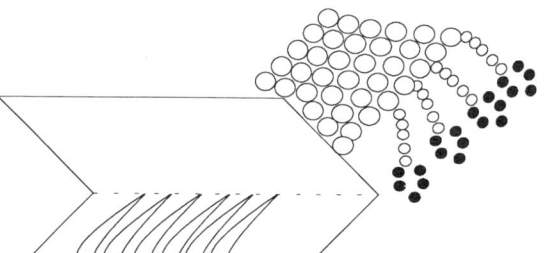

Fig. 18. The piece is removed from the loom and the warp pairs are brought through a piece of leather. Warp pairs are then tied together.

3. Sew one-half of a snap to the leather. Then fold the leather in half and glue the two sides together using Tandy's Barge Cement or E-6000 glue, hiding all the thread ends and stitches.

4. After the glue has dried, trim the edges of the leather and overcast them neatly. As you overcast the edge, you may wish to pick up a bead with each stitch for a more decorative edge.

5. Do the same to the warp threads on the other end.

Fig. 19. Finished leather closure with beads sewn to the edge.

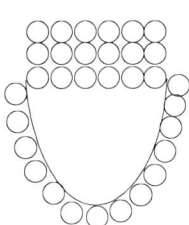

Congratulations! Your Sea Anemone Bracelet is complete!

Other Books on Beadwork

Only a few good books on beadwork have come to my attention although many publications have a section devoted to just one or two techniques. Here are my suggestions for books. These books and others are available from Beautiful Beads, 115 Hennepin Avenue, Minneapolis, MN 55401. (Prices subject to change.)

"Contemporary Beadwork I: Counted and Charted Patterns for Flat Peyote Stitch," by Diane Fitzgerald, $19.95

"Beads & Threads: A New Technique for Fiber Jewelry," by Diane Fitzgerald and Helen Banes, $37.95

"Those Bad, Bad Beads" by Virginia Blakelock, $16.00.

"Indian Bead-Weaving Patterns" by Horace Goodhue, $9.95.

"The New Beadwork" by Alice Scherer and Kathleen Moss, $24.95.

Please add $3.00 per book for postage and handling.

A sturdy wooden bead loom similar to that shown in the illustrations is available for $24.95 plus $3.00 for shipping and handling.

For further information on beadwork, contact:

The Center for the Study of Beadwork
PO Box 13719
Portland, OR 97213
or
Bead & Button Magazine
PO Box 4520
Seattle, WA 98104

Sources of Supplies

There are many sources of beads, thread, needles and supplies listed in Ornament Magazine which is available on many newsstands or by subscription. Write to:

> Ornament Magazine
> P.O. Box 2349
> San Marcos, CA 92079-9806

ISBN 0-9646077-1